SUCCEED ANYWAY!

The Entrepreneur Development Manual

Tauheed S. Burke

PAGE PUBLISHING, INC.
Conneaut Lake, PA

First originally published by Page Publishing 2020

ISBN 978-1-66240-213-5 (pbk)
ISBN 978-1-66240-296-8 (hc)
ISBN 978-1-66240-214-2 (digital)

Printed in the United States of America

Dedication:

This manual is dedicated to my loving Grandmother, my Brother Dougie Burke, and my three Sons, Torrey, Tauheed and Tahj Burke. You have been and are my inspiration.

Entrepreneur Development Program!

This manual is intended for students and young adults who feel deep down inside there is more to life then working 40 years for someone else and not experience the Quality of Life they deserve. In these pages you will learn the concepts of entrepreneurship.

YOUR JOURNEY BEGINS..........NOW

Contents

CHAPTER 1

My Journey

You don't have to come from somewhere
special to do something special.

—TB

I GREW UP in a place called Cherry Hill in Baltimore, Maryland. I was the oldest boy in our family. My father was not in my life, so I had to find a way to be head of the family. We had very little to no money. I never could do the things my friends did. My mom was not in a position to afford anything other than the essentials to survive. I remember when I was around ten years old, all the kids in the neighborhood had signed up for Boy Scouts. I was so excited to join.

When I went home to ask my mother, she said, "I don't have the money." I was so hurt. I remember it like it was yesterday. I sat down and asked myself, "Why does it have to be this way?" My mother used to say, "I can't wait until you get eighteen and get on your own…," I said respectfully, "Me either, you will see!" When I made that statement, I felt obligated to find a way to deliver. I said, "I don't know how, but I'm not going to continue to live like this!"

At the time, I started doing whatever I had to do to survive. My mom never understood why I was so different. She thought I was a renegade. Instead, I just wanted a better life for myself. Although I got into a lot of legal trouble as a child, I always made it a priority to go to school and excel in sports. Sports helped me become competitive, helped me learn how to win, and helped me become a leader.

I always had a dream; I knew there was something better than what I was experiencing. When I was a kid, I used to watch *The Lifestyle of the Rich and Famous*. I watched as Robin Leach talked about the yachts, the fancy hotels, restaurants, and quality of life. Although I never physically saw it, I lived it in my mind, and I knew, somehow, I would have it.

There were three turning points in my life as a child. The first one was when I was fifteen. There was myself and about fifteen of my friends, walking from the shopping center in Cherry Hill. One of my friends asked everyone: "Do you wanna get high?" I was the only one who asked, "Off what?" They said, "Dope." I asked, "You mean shoot dope?" My friend said, "Yes." I also was the only one who said, "Hell *no*!" Because I was an athlete, I was reluctant to abuse my body to that extent. I saw too many people I looked up to and admired take a major fall as a result of being on drugs. Of course, when I said "no," my friends called me all types of names. I said, "I will be whatever you want me to be! But I am not doing that!" When I walked away as I was dribbling my basketball, I had no clue how all our lives would change forever. Most of them are dead, in jail, or strung out on drugs. I had no clue how devastating that moment was to my friends I loved.

The second turning point was when I had my son, Torrey Burke, at age sixteen. I knew that if I was going to raise a child to become a man that I had to change my ways. He was the biggest blessing that ever happened to me! He forced me to change; although change did not take place immediately.

The third turning point happened in downtown Baltimore. I was hanging out with my good friend, Big Warren. We decided to go to Lexington Terrace, the location of the hit series, *The Wire*. I never watched that show…because we lived it! While we were there, we got ambushed by some of our most hated rivals—ambushed at gunpoint! Thank God we were able to walk away. I wanted to retaliate. The next day I contacted all my friends. We set up a meeting at my home. The meeting was while my mom was at work. We were making plans to retaliate. My friends were down 100 percent for making a move on the gang who ambushed us. My friends took the decision very seriously because they knew it was not acceptable for us to let them get away with what happened. All of a sudden, something hit me. I then went upstairs to use the restroom.

While in the restroom, it seemed like God entered the room and started asking me questions: "Are you really about to do this? If you do, you will never ever be able to turn back. What about your son?" I dropped to my knees and stayed there for about one minute, which seemed like hours. I then got up and looked in the mirror. The two options and the vision of the results of both options flashed in front of me: the option to call it off or the option to retaliate. The option to call it off would have bought a pleasant ending. The option to retaliate would be devastating to all involved. I got myself together, walked downstairs to face my friends/mob, and called it off.

I painted a picture for them of why. They were very pissed at me; however, I could see that deep down a few of them understood why I chose not to. As they left my home, they were shaking their heads. Still finding ways to get into trouble, a few weeks later, my friends and I were a contributing factor to a major riot that took place at my high school. Word got back to security that our gang started the riot. When I walked into the school building the next day, the head of security and the principle were waiting for Big Warren and me. They apprehended both of us, and we both got arrested and expelled from school. To make manners worse, it was during my junior year, in the middle of the basketball season. Now my dream of getting a scholarship were done. As time went by, I was trying to figure everything out. Somehow my mom got me accepted into Southwestern High School in West Baltimore, with about three months left in the school year. In order to make it to school on time, I had to get up at 5:30 a.m. to catch two buses on my own and be to school by 8:00 every morning. With a determination not to fail, I worked extremely hard and found a way to advance to the twelfth grade.

With a lot of time on my hands during the time I was expelled, I made a decision that it was now time to start the process of change. I started isolating myself from all my friends. I started being by myself, working on myself, working on my mind and body. My twelfth-grade year I made the honor roll while being a star basketball player. I graduated from high school and was accepted into Cheney State University, near Philadelphia, Pennsylvania. The challenge was that I only stayed for three days and left. (To be discussed in my next book.) Five days later I joined the United States Navy. Although I enjoyed the Navy, my first twelve months were quite challenging. I had to get adjusted to a totally different way of life. I spent seven years of my life in the Military. I started my first entrepreneur experience while still enlisted. The Navy helped me create the discipline, experience, and mental toughness to start putting it all together. When I left the Military, I went directly into business full-time. I have never in my adult life been on a job interview. By the will of God and my desire to achieve, I have always been in business for myself. Through all the adversities and struggles along the journey, I have truly been living the American Dream, and it's just the beginning.

From the Eyes of My Sister

My brother is always driven. Something inside of him pushed him even when things seemed impossible. I saw the following traits in him that has shaped his success today:

Sought Mentors

Because we were raised without a father figure, my brother always sought out mentors in our community. The gentlemen he chose were older and were making a powerful impact in our community.

Early Development of Entrepreneur and Leadership Skills

He always said, "When I grow up, I am going to be a businessman."

I use to call my brother and Torrey's (his son) mom Bonnie and Clyde. They always had some kind of scheme cooking for making money. They would sell clothes, handbags, or whatever they could to turn a profit. Sometimes he would get me wrapped up doing the wrong things.

At the age of fifteen, he showed pronounced leadership skills. He would organize his friends to do the craziest things. What was even crazier is that after he pitched his motivational speech, his gang of fourteen and fifteen-year-olds ran off, excited to do whatever crazy things he came with to make money.

When he was fifteen, my second-to-the-youngest brother and I saw the money rolling in. Keep in mind we didn't have any money. I rarely remember having $1 in my pocket. We found out where my brother stashed his cash, so we figured he wouldn't mind sharing. Tauheed noticed his stash was going down. He was upset and could do nothing but tell my mother that we were helping ourselves to his funds. Without his permission. My mom said, "Get a bank account," and Tauheed said, "But Mom, I am only fifteen years old. I can't open an account." She said, "Open one anyway." My brother and I stood in the background, laughing. So I think at that point he learned how to manage and really hide his cash. My brother and I never found his stash of cash again.

Defeated the Odds

I was worried about my brother when we were teenagers. I was worried that he would end up in jail or worse. So many of his friends did end up dead, incarcerated, or addicts. On several occasions he had to appear before a judge; however, the last time he had to appear, I don't remember why. I do remember it was serious. We all were scared. What I do know is that it was his last time he ever got in trouble with the law. You see, my mother always fussed about having to sit on the hard court benches as a result of his errors. That last time he was blessed because he was just under eighteen.

After that last court appearance, he made a miraculous change. I noticed he started distancing himself from his friends. That was the real journey to change, which is, "if you want a change, then change the people around you." That's when his real journey began. You see, despite all the extra activities after school, he never missed school.

Him and I, no matter what was going on, we found a way to get to school every day. During the course of our high school years, both of us got suspended for a long period of time. My mother didn't have to punish us. We punished ourselves. When we got back to school, we worked extra hard and was still able to graduate on time.

Driven…

My mom and her friend drove him to college, and there was a problem with his dorm assignment. He didn't have a place to stay. Mind you, we were broke. There was no way my mother was able to afford an outside apartment for him. Most would have given up and hit the streets again or settle for a minimum-wage job. He got off the streets and joined the US Navy.

He is driven. I remember him getting really serious about Primerica, but he did not have a car. At the time, I was in the Navy and about to deploy to Yokosuka, Japan. So I sold him his very first and my very first car. It was a burgundy-and-brown two-tone Chevy Chevette. Every time I picture him in that car, I laugh.

The Results

During the Reagan era, recreation centers and after-school programs were cut in our neighborhood. Those recreation centers were the life blood for my brother and I when we were growing up. It provided an outlet for many youths to play sports and socialize.

I remember him saying after all the closures were said and done, "When I get enough money, I am going to come back into the neighborhood and help rebuild." He held true to his promise. He has accomplished the following that I know of: coached and sponsored youth sports, mentored male youth, and he is helping to rehabilitate Baltimore housing one vacant home at a time. And last but not least, he started "The Cherry Hill Hall of Fame." Where he honored individuals in the community. Where despite the odds, they exceeded expectations and become role models, supported the community and or became successful. There has never been a community in this country that have developed a Hall of Fame, except for the Cherry hill community, started by my brother.

Finally, this is what I learned from my little Brother, "Succeed Any Way" Your skill set may not be that of an entrepreneur, but Succeed Any Way.

CHAPTER 2

Mindset Development

Without a mindset change, money is insignificant
—TB

Section 1: Mindset

I BELIEVE THE most important attribute that helped most successful people achieve success is faith and belief in one's self. When
I was a child, I always thought differently. I could not understand
it…nor did my mother understand. I felt like I was meant to be
somebody. I had no reason to believe that because I had no evidence
of anyone in my neighborhood that was living the way I felt life
should be lived. When I was sixteen, I started studying progressive
Americans. I changed my diet. When I went into the Navy, I spent
many months on a ship in the middle of the ocean; therefore, I had
time to think about what I wanted in life. I made a sound decision
that I would win! I created a journal. I started reading on various
topics: religion, politics, success, finances, and more. At the point I
began reading those subjects, I discovered the key ingredient to success: *self-development.*

Section 2: Master Self

1. *Spiritual*: Despite your religious belief, I feel it is important to spend time in prayer and meditation. Spend time thanking the higher power. The number-one key to success is to have total belief that God will not let you down. Once you believe that God has your back, you will go after what you want 100 percent without hesitation or doubt. A lot of people make the mistake of thinking that all the good that happens is because of them. No matter how successful you become in life, always remember: *all praise is due to God.*

2. *Mental Growth*: You have to work on your thinking every day. When I was a child, there was so much negativity around me. I saw people get murdered. I saw people get robbed. I got robbed! I saw people shoot drugs in front of me. You name it, I saw it. I had to find a way to be happy and not to allow the environment to overtake me. Once I became eighteen, I had to leave Baltimore City. If I didn't, I would have become a statistic. Watching the news, being around negative people, reading negative stories, thinking about the past, and worrying about the future will cripple you. The only moment you can control is the present moment. Focus your attention on the now; easier said than done. However, once you can control your thinking, you can control your happiness. Read God's Word, read positive books, have positive conversations, never talk about others, watch videos, listen to CDs, go on YouTube to study successful people and study their habits. If you find yourself in a negative environment, do yourself a favor and *leave*!

3. *Physical*: What's the use of making a lot of money if you're not healthy enough to enjoy it? Unfortunately, that important factor is often overlooked. One plan, which has been effective for me, is having a weekly schedule where I spend time strengthening my body working on cardio, muscle-toning, and more. Watch what you eat while limiting salt, sugar, white bread, red meat, sodas, cigarettes, drugs,

and liquor. All these items are toxic and will contribute to lack of focus, concentration, laziness, ill health, overweight, and premature aging. Preserve your body—you only have one. Just think, with all the success you will have, I'm sure you want to look lean, mean, and beautiful in your extensive wardrobe.

4. *Entertainment*: Most people think that they have to wait until they get to a certain place or financial status in life in order to start enjoying themselves. What I have discovered is that life is a continuum—you never get to that place because life continues to evolve. You will evolve. What you think you want when you are sixteen will change when you are twenty-two. What you think is success today won't seem that way later in life.

5. I used to tell myself, once I make a million dollars, I will buy myself a Rolls Royce or Bentley. Although I love those cars, once I made that million, I decided there were more important things to do instead of buying a $160,000 car.

6. The most profound advice I can give is to enjoy the moment. Enjoy the struggle. Take time every month and reward yourself to a nice dinner, a Broadway play, a jazz concert, a one-day excursion. Every ninety days take a trip, even if it's for only three days. Every thirty days do something that benefits others. As John Maxwell says, "The joy is the journey, and the journey is the joy."

7. When I started my business, I was a single parent. I had to reward my sons for me not being home all week. So every Friday we went out to dinner. Every Sunday we went to the basketball court. I made sure, even to this day, that I reward my hard work with a good quality of life. I highly recommend that you do the same in pursuit of your dreams. Treat yourself while you are in the hunt because, for winners, it really never stops. The hunt for greatness is a lifetime journey.

8. *Financial:* When you go into business for yourself, if all you focus on is the money, you will never grow. Don't get

it twisted; you must make money as a business owner. It may take years to build a solid operation, but it doesn't take years to become profitable. Making money along the way gives you confidence that what you are building is working. Saving money along the way gives you the security, peace of mind, and ammunition to deal with unforeseen business adversity. (See chapter on money management.)

Section 3: Five Stages of Life

Something interesting happened to me on February 7, 2020.

While I was on vacation, I was sitting at a restaurant with a friend. It was a table of five, and there were two empty seats next to us.

An older couple slowly walked up to me and said, "Is someone sitting in those seats?"

I said, "No, you guys are more than welcome to sit here."

They gladly sat down, as the older man slouched down in his chair half asleep, his wife was sitting across from him; at the time they really were not saying much. Well, a gorgeous woman walked by. The old man put his head up and followed her with his eyes to her seat.

I overheard his wife say jokingly, "*That woke you up and got your attention, didn't it?*"

I had to laugh out loud, and they both looked over at me and started laughing as well. He and his wife started talking about various topics, and he said to her, "See, we have to enjoy ourselves because we only have five stages of life." I was looking away as if I was not paying attention.

As he started talking about the stages, I said, "Sir, I am sorry to interrupt you, however, what you are saying is so profound. Is it possible you can give me the stages so I can write them down? I am finalizing a book, and I would love to add these statements."

He said, sure, because his voice was not the strongest. I asked if it was okay to move my chair close to his so I could hear him clearly. Below are Vernon and Lucia, his wife. Five Stages of Life. Nice meeting you, and thank you so much for sharing your insight with me.

Stage 1—This the beginning stage, the day we are blessed to be born.

Stage 2—The process of life begins: being a child, starting school, going through the challenges of learning about life, completing the cycle of education.

Stage 3—Go into the workforce, creating your means of making and saving money, taking on responsibilities, and building a family. Stage 3 can be the longest stage of life. It could take up to thirty years.

Stage 4—One should have built success and be accomplished. Your activity may decrease. The hard work on a daily basis to make money should have stopped. You should start enjoying the fruits of your labor.

Stage 5—Could be the shortest stage of life. However, you should be able to live and do whatever you choose, travel the world, have the means to help others in need, provide leadership and mentorship. Enjoy the memories and every moment because, unfortunately, it will not last too much longer.

My conclusion: Each stage of life is what we make it. Live, learn, and enjoy it.

Section 4: Purpose, Belief, and Adversity

Once you make a decision that you want to own your own business, you have to decide your purpose. My good friend, Walter Charles, always says: "*When purpose is not known, misuse is inevitable.*" Your purpose will drive you when nothing else will. My purpose was to have a better quality of life, deliver for my mom and children, travel the world, and impact my community; that's what I thought about every day. I visualized how that would feel and how it would look. Frustration and setbacks were simply for me to overcome because I was driven.

Everybody wants to make over a million dollars a year. However, few are willing to pay $15,000 per week in payroll. If you want success, in any field, you must pay the price, upfront, in advance—no discount, no layaway. Adversity must be your friend. Before I went to the next level in income and success, I was challenged majorly at the current level. Life is not fair. In life there will be things that appear to be good but aren't good for you. Some things may appear to be bad but are good for you.

The haters will be among you, and you must ignore them. *Do not let the fans in the stands take you off course.* People will try to tear you down any way they can. Always do your best to be a good person. Although you are not perfect, do not ever worry about what others think and say about you.

Do not wait until you become perfect before you believe you can start. If you do that, that day will never come. Most successful people are not perfect, and they know it; they focus on what is good and appreciate what God has blessed them with and make the best of it. I challenge you to do the same.

Before you become a leader, you will be challenged physically, mentally, spiritually, and financially. Work on your mind every day so that you will be prepared.

One of the biggest hurdles I had to overcome was in 1993 when I made my first $100,000 in a year. That year, interestingly, was the worst beginning one could have encountered. My best friend ever in life was my little brother, Dougie Burke. He had an eating disorder that caused him to overeat. There was a program at Walter P. Canter, one of the only ones in the country. Well, in 1991 the program was closed, and from that point forward, my brother's health started to slowly fade. My mom did everything she could to find a location that would help him—but to no avail. In 1993 he passed away. The devastation of not seeing him again was overwhelming.

Also, in the middle of 1993, I almost lost my home, my freedom, and my top income producer left the company. I had no cash flow coming in for eight months. One of my friends said, "You should sell your home." I started looking in the paper to see if I could find a good job. After doing deep, deep thinking and praying, I decided that it would take time to find a job; and then when I find one, it would take three weeks to get paid, and the pay would not be enough. If I sold my home, we would have nowhere to live, and I did not believe I had enough money to buy another one. I then came up with a plan.

I decided to rent my basement for the same amount as my mortgage. I was not going to get a JOB (just over broke). I was going to take it one day at a time. I was going to use the setbacks to drive me. I put my brother's picture in my office. I looked at it every day, and every time I felt it was getting tough, I said to myself, "I am not going through anything more challenging then what he faced." So I locked in; nobody in my business or my personal life knew the major challenges I was facing. It was between God, me, and my dreams of doing something special for my children, my family, and community. Once I locked in, I came up with a business plan to grow my company, my cash flow, and myself. I went from making $0 income the first eight months of 1993 to $108,000 by December 31, 1993. I worked from 9:00 a.m. until 9:00 p.m. every day except Saturday and Sunday. During the weekend, I would put in about four hours per day. The rest of the weekend was devoted to hanging out with my sons and finding ways to have fun.

When I made my first $100,000 that year, my mentor, Andy Young said, "Now that you made $100,000, you are in a position to start your journey to financial freedom. It doesn't mean you will—it means you have a shot." What he meant was that I developed the mental toughness to start the process. *Let adversity be your friend!*

CHAPTER 3

History of Philanthropists and Trailblazers

*Most never understand the power of
the moment until it's in the past.*

—TB

THIS CHAPTER IS designed to show accomplishments of philanthropist and trailblazers who were instrumental in empowering individuals and generations.

You have to believe that despite your current situation and circumstances, you still can succeed. We cannot use our ethnicity as an excuse. There is a history of success in various cultures that may not be present in the currently used history books. I challenge you to spend time researching your history. You will find that there is a rich history of success...despite your nationality.

Black Wall Street

In the early 1900s there existed a thriving community comprised black-owned businesses in Tulsa, Oklahoma. For many in that Greenwood neighborhood, their Black Wall Street represented security for themselves and their families. There were bustling theaters, schools, entertainment establishments, and a strong sense pride as its middle and upper class saw strong wealth. Such togetherness was born out of many years of segregation and discrimination. Black Wall Street presented a way to find strength despite a majority society that restricted its growth and freedom. This strong community of some ten thousand African Americans paved the way for black communities and businesses to strive.

Yes, there were other primarily majority black communities during that time. What set Black Wall Street apart was its ability to support each other through education, easy access to healthcare, employment opportunities, and economic and money-growth education.

Inevitably, many in predominantly white communities were infuriated by the better economic opportunities bestowed upon their neighboring African Americans. They started spreading hatred and falsely accused them of crimes that were not committed. With hatred in their heart, they sought to tear down Black Wall Street. What better way to insight a hate-filled racist group then to accuse the "enemy" of sexual assault upon one their own. With that smoldering hatred, lynch mobs formed, and over two thousand KKK members sought justice. Black businesses were burned, homes destroyed, lives were lost, and fear engulfed what was left of Greenwood. To make matters worse, the government blamed its residences and made it nearly impossible to rebuild. Building a new Black Wall Street is probable. What will it take? It will take a united people with a common goal of economic strength for its community.

Black Wall Street, a well-documented dark part of history, serves as a lesson that pride and opportunity can happen by circulating money within your own community and doing business with one another. Let that ancestral drive propel you to invest in each other.

Andrew Carnegie

A Scottish-American industrialist, business magnate, and philanthropist. Carnegie led the expansion of the American steel industry in the late 19th century and became one of the richest Americans in history. He became a leading philanthropist in the United States and in the British Empire. During the last 18 years of his life, he gave away $350 million (conservatively $65 billion in 2019 dollars, based on percentage of GDP) to charities, foundations, and universities—almost 90 percent of his fortune. His 1889 article proclaiming "The Gospel of Wealth" called on the rich to use their wealth to improve society, and stimulated a wave of philanthropy.

Carnegie was born in Dunfermline, Scotland, and immigrated to the United States with his parents in 1848 at age 12. Carnegie started work as a telegrapher, and by the 1860s had investments in railroads, railroad sleeping cars, bridges, and oil derricks. He accumulated further wealth as a bond salesman, raising money for American enterprise in Europe. He built Pittsburgh's Carnegie Steel Company, which he sold to J. P. Morgan in 1901 for $303,450,000. It became the U.S. Steel Corporation. After selling Carnegie Steel, he surpassed John D. Rockefeller as the richest American for the next several years.

Carnegie devoted the remainder of his life to large-scale philanthropy, with special emphasis on local libraries, world peace, education, and scientific research. With the fortune he made from business, he built Carnegie Hall in New York, NY, and the Peace Palace and founded the Carnegie Corporation of New York, Carnegie Endowment for International Peace, Carnegie Institution for Science, Carnegie Trust for the Universities of Scotland, Carnegie Hero Fund, Carnegie Mellon University, and the Carnegie Museums of Pittsburgh, among others.

Bilal ibn Rabah

Born in Mecca, in AD 580, Bilal ibn Rabah, aka Bilal ibn Riyah, was a former slave. His father was an Arab slave, and his mother was a princess of Ethiopia who was captured. Bilal was of a handsome and impressive stature, dark-brown complexion with sparkling eyes, a fine nose, and bright skin. He was also gifted with a deep, melodious, resonant voice. He wore a beard, which was thin on both cheeks. He was endowed with great wisdom and a sense of dignity and self-esteem. Through hard work, Bilal became recognized as a good slave and was entrusted with the keys to the Idols of Arabia. However, racism and sociopolitical statutes of Arabia prevented Bilal from achieving a lofty position in society

He listened to the teachings of Muhammad and converted to Islam. Upon learning this, his master, Umayyah ibn Khalaf, beat and tortured him by dragging him through Mecca and stretching him by ropes to break his faith. Instead of breaking, Bilal would repeat, "*Ahad, Ahad*" (God is absolute/one). Word reached Muhammad, and he bought Bilal's freedom. Bilal later rose to prominence in the Islamic State of Medina as Muhammad appointed him minister of the *Bayt al-Mal* (treasury). In this capacity, Bilal distributed funds to widows, orphans, wayfarers, and others who could not support themselves. Because of his deep clear voice, he was made the first Muezzin (caller to prayer) of Islam.

Bilal died around AD 640. His descendants, the Mandinka clan, migrated to Mali in West Africa. From the Mali empire emerged King Mansa Musa, one of the richest men who ever lived.

Mansa Musa of Mali

Mansa Musa (c. 1280–c. 1337) was the tenth Mansa—sultan, emperor, his leadership of Mali, a state which stretched across two thousand miles from the Atlantic Ocean to Lake Chad and which included all or parts of the modern nations of Mauritania, Senegal, Gambia, Guinea, Burkina Faso, Mali, Niger, Nigeria, and Chad—who ensured decades of peace and prosperity in Western Africa.

Mansa Musa captured the attention of the Arab world when he became the first Muslim ruler in West Africa to make the nearly four-thousand-mile journey to make a pilgrimage to the Muslim holy city of Mecca in 1324. Unlike his grandfather *Sundiata*, Mansa Musa was a devout Muslim. He was also knowledgeable in Arabic. This pilgrimage introduced him to rulers in the Middle East and in Europe.

Preparing for the expedition took years and involved the work of artisans in numerous towns and cities across Mali. In 1324 Musa began his pilgrimage with a train of thousands of richly dressed escorts. His entourage included soldiers, civilians, and slaves, five hundred heralds bearing gold staffs and dressed in fine silks, and many camels and horses bearing an abundance of gold bars. Musa made generous donations to the poor and to charitable organizations, as well as the rulers of the lands his entourage crossed. On his stop in Cairo, Egypt, the emperor gave out so much gold he generated a brief decline in its value. It took Cairo's gold market a decade to recover.

Musa built houses in Cairo and in Mecca to house his attendants, and as he traveled the world, a lot of people, notably the merchants of Venice, saw him in Alexandria and returned to Italy with tales of Mansa Musa's ridiculous wealth, which helped create the myth in the minds of Europeans that West Africa was a land of gold, an El Dorado.

Upon his return from Mecca, Mansa Musa brought Arab scholars, government bureaucrats, and architects. Among those who returned with him was the architect Ishaq El Teudjin who introduced advanced building techniques to Mali.

Mansa Musa was enamored of structures. He brought architects from Spain and Cairo to build his grand palace in Timbuktu, which he conquered with Gao on his way to Mecca. In addition, he built the Hall of Audience and the University of Sankore, which became a center of learning and culture, drawing scholars from around Africa and the Middle East.

By the end of his reign, the Sankore University was fully staffed with a library with the largest collection of books in Africa. At the time of his death, he was a man of tremendous wealth. *People Magazine* estimated his wealth at over $400 billion!

Cesar Chavez

Born in Yuma, Arizona, on March 27, 1927, Cesar Chavez was a manual laborer and enlisted in the Navy for two years. He moved to California, married, and became involved with the Community Service Organization (CSO). Through it, he welcomed an opportunity to help laborers register to vote; many of whom, like him, were of Mexican-American heritage. In 1952 he became the organization's national director. In 1962 he left CSO and cofounded United Farm Workers (UFW) and over time became the best-known Latino American civil rights activist. Because of his leadership and ability to mobilize people, popular American labor movements sought him out to help increase their Hispanic enrolment. He was the voice for the struggling farm worker, and nationwide attention was given to his nonviolent tactics. By the early 1970s, the UFW boasted fifty thousand field-workers in California and Florida.

In his later life, Chavez became an advocate for veganism. On April 23, 1993, he died and quickly became a major icon in the Latino-American community. Many schools, parks, and streets were named after him. He also became an icon for organized labor and Hispanic empowerment beginning at the grassroots level. One of his popular slogans was "Si, se puede," which is Spanish for "Yes, it can be done." This was adopted as the 2008 slogan for Barack Obama, "Yes, we can!" In 1994, years after his death, Chavez posthumously received the Presidential Medal of Freedom, and several states recognize March 31, the anniversary of his birth, as Cesar Chavez Day.

Madam C.J. Walker

A black female, born in 1867, which became a millionaire, sounds impossible! However, it did happen. Sarah Breedlove who, in later life, adopted the name Madam C. J. Walker, accomplished just that.

Sarah Breedlove was the eldest child born after the Emancipation Proclamation. Her parents were slaves and became an orphan at age seven. At age fourteen, she married Moses McWilliams and widowed at age twenty with a daughter. Upon the death of her husband, she and her child moved to St. Louis Missouri to be with her older brothers, who were barbers.

She worked as a washerwoman for a decade and was a member of St. Paul African Methodist Church. She found many mentors and sang in the choir. During that time, she tried various commercial hair products and began to experiment with her own formula to cure scalp infections that caused baldness. In 1905 she moved to Denver and worked as a cook for a pharmacist. From him she learned basic chemistry and was able to perfect an ointment that healed dandruff and other hygiene-related ailments. She continued to perfect hair-care formulas.

In July 1906 she married Charles Walker and became known as Madam C.J. Walker. (Madam was adopted from women pioneers of the French beauty industry.) Her husband, who was also her business partner, advertised and promoted her products. Those products were sold door to door and taught other black women how to groom and style their hair. Her daughter handled the mail-ordering while she and her husband traveled throughout the east and south to expand the business. She developed "The Walker System," which was a method of grooming designed to promote hair growth and condition the scalp

Over time Madam CJ Walker had developed and manufactured various hair-care products, established hair-care training center. In addition to training in sales and grooming, Walker showed other black women how to budget, build their own businesses, and encouraged them to become financially independent.

Walker owned several cars, including a Ford Model T and a Waverly, an electric car. She also had a personal, full-time chauffeur.

Walker died on May 25, 1919. At the time of her death, she was considered to be the wealthiest African-American woman in America. Her estate was estimated to be $600,000 (about $8 million in present-day dollars). At the time of her death, the average

American's annual salary was $750 (about $50,000 in present-day dollars).

John F. Kennedy

John Fitzgerald Kennedy (May 29, 1917— November 22, 1963) an American politician who served as the 35th *president of the United States.* Kennedy served at the height of the *Cold War*, and the majority of his work as president concerned relations with the Soviet Union and Cuba. A Democrat, Kennedy represented Massachusetts in the U.S. House of Representatives and Senate prior to becoming president.

Kennedy was born into a wealthy, political family in Brookline, Massachusetts. He graduated from Harvard University in 1940, before joining the U.S. Naval Reserve the following year. During World War II, he commanded a series of PT boats in the Pacific theater and earned the Navy and Marine Corps Medal for his service. After the war, Kennedy represented the 11th congressional district of Massachusetts in the U.S. House of Representatives from 1947 to 1953. He was subsequently elected to the U.S. Senate and served as the junior Senator from Massachusetts from 1953 to 1960. While in the Senate, Kennedy published his book *Profiles in Courage,* which won a Pulitzer Prize. In the 1960 presidential election, he narrowly defeated Republican opponent Richard Nixon, who was the incumbent vice president.

Kennedy's administration included high tensions with communist states in the Cold War. He increased the number of American military advisers in South Vietnam. In April 1961, he authorized an attempt to overthrow the Cuban government of Fidel Castro in the Bay of Pigs Invasion. Kennedy authorized the Cuban Project in November 1961. He rejected Operation Northwoods (plans for false flag attacks to gain approval for a war against Cuba) in March 1962. However, his administration continued to plan for an invasion of Cuba in the summer of 1962. The following October, U.S. spy planes discovered Soviet missile bases had been deployed in Cuba; the resulting period of tensions, termed the Cuban Missile Crisis, nearly resulted in the breakout of a global thermonuclear conflict. The Strategic Hamlet Program began in Vietnam during his presidency. Domestically, Kennedy presided over the establishment of the Peace Corps and the continuation of the Apollo space program,

Although he was born into wealth, JFK fought hard for the common man. He was a champion of, and defender of, civil rights. He viewed it as moral, constitutional, and legal. Before, during, his presidency, racial tension was rampant and minority races, particularly African-Americans, faced daily discrimination. Civil unrest was rampant, lynching was commonplace, and murderous mobs felt empowered by corrupt law enforcement that often turned a blind eye. JFK pushed for the passage of major civil rights legislation submitted to Congress. He fought hard to end racial discrimination of African-Americans. After his death, Congress enacted many of his proposals, including the Civil Rights Act. Kennedy ranks highly in polls of U.S. presidents with historians and the general public. His personal life has also been the focus of considerable sustained interest.

Bass Reeves

Bass Reeves was born a slave in Arkansas in 1838. His slave master, William S. Reeves, moved the household to Texas in 1846. When the Civil War broke out, William Reeves' son George was made a colonel in the Confederate army and took Bass to war with him. At the most opportune moment, Reeves escaped while George was sleeping and took off out west for Indian Territory. Accounts vary on whether Bass beat up George as he left, and whether his immediate aim was freedom or to escape punishment over a card game dispute. In any case, Reeves went to live among the Creek and Seminole Indians. He learned their customs and languages and became a proficient territorial scout. Reeves eventually procured a homestead in Van Buren, Arkansas, where he was the first black settler. He married Nellie Jennie, built an eight-room house with his bare hands, and raised ten children—five girls and five boys. Life was good, but it was about to change for Bass Reeves. The state of Oklahoma at the time was two different territories: Oklahoma Territory and Indian Territory. Indian Territory was where the Creek, Cherokee, Choctaw, Seminole, and Chickasaw tribes who were forcibly removed from their homes were resettled following the Indian Removal Act of 1830. But they weren't the only citizens of Indian Territory. There were also former slaves of the tribes, freed and made tribal members after the Civil War, settlers from the East (both black and white) who sharecropped tribal property, and a good measure of outlaws fleeing from civilization. Indian territory was attractive to lawbreakers because of its peculiar judiciary arrangement: The tribal courts had jurisdiction only over tribal members. Non-Indians were under the jurisdiction of federal courts, but there were few marshals to supervise a very large area.

In 1875, "Hanging Judge" Isaac C. Parker was made the federal judge of Indian Territory. One of his first acts was to make James Fagan a U.S. Marshal and order him to hire 200 deputies. Fagan knew of Reeves and his ability to negotiate Indian Territory and speak the languages, so Reeves was named the first black Deputy Marshal west of the Mississippi. As such, he was authorized to arrest both black and white lawbreakers. Reeves was well aware of the historic precedent, and took his responsibilities seriously.

Reeves was 38 years old at the time, 6 feet 2 inches tall, weighed 180 pounds, and rode a large horse. He cut an imposing figure as he patrolled the 75,000 square miles of Indian Territory. He quickly gained a reputation as a tough and fearless lawman who managed to bring in outlaws thought to be invincible. Reeves traveled the long circuit with a wagon, cook, and often a posse. He carried chains to secure prisoners to the wagon, as he sometimes had a dozen or more by the time he returned to Ft. Smith, where Judge Parker held court.

In 1882, Reeves arrested Belle Starr for horse theft. Some accounts say that she turned herself in when she heard that the legendary Bass Reeves was looking for her.

In 1889, after Reeves was assigned to Paris, Texas, he went after the Tom Story gang for their long-term horse theft operation. He waited along the route Tom Story used, and surprised him with an arrest warrant. Story panicked and drew his gun, but Reeves drew and shot him dead before Story could fire. The rest of the gang disbanded and were never heard from again.

Reeves approached the three murderous Brunter brothers and handed them a warrant for their arrest. The three outlaws laughed and read the warrant, and in the split second they all took their eyes off Reeves, he managed to draw his gun and kill two of them, and immediately disarmed and arrested the third.

Although Reeves was a skilled frontiersman and spoke several languages, he had never learned to read. Once, when two potential assassins forced Reeves off his horse, he asked them for one last request—that someone read him a letter from his wife. When the outlaws were momentarily distracted by the piece of paper they were handed, Reeves drew his gun and turned the situation around. The second outlaw dropped his gun in surprise, and they were both arrested. Reeves used the "piece of paper" ruse several times in his career to distract felons to similar ends.

Reeves was arrested himself in 1887, and charged with murder in the death of his posse cook, William Leach. Brought to trial before Judge Parker, he testified that he shot the cook by accident while cleaning his gun, and was acquitted.

The marshal was famous for fair-mindedness and was impossible to bribe or corrupt. In 1902 he arrested his own son, Benny, for murdering his wife (Reeves' daughter-in-law). Benny had fled to the badlands after the crime, and no other marshal was willing to pursue him. As distasteful as the task was, Reeves brought him back, and Benny served twenty years at Leavenworth. Oklahoma became a state in 1907, and Reeves' commission as marshal ended. He was 68 years old by then, but took on another position with the Muskogee Police Department, which he kept until his health began to fail. Reeves died of Bright's disease in 1910. In his 32 years as a Deputy U.S. Marshal, Reeves had seen bullets fly through his clothing and hat, but was never injured by an outlaw. His record of 3,000 arrests dwarfs the arrest records of better known Old West lawmen such as Bat Masterson, Wyatt Earp, and Wild Bill Hickok.

The story of Bass Reeves is sometimes cited as the inspiration for *The Lone Ranger*. It also may have been an inspiration for the film *Django Unchained*. The 2010 straight-to-video movie *Bass Reeves* is a fictionalized account of the lawman's life. In 2011, the bridge that connects Muskogee and Fort Gibson in Oklanahoma was named the Bass Reeves Memorial Bridge.

CHAPTER 4

Money-Management Principles

AVOID SPENDING MONEY until you have saved a portion of your earnings. Do not pay any bills until you have paid yourself first. If you get into this habit, you will force yourself to adapt the beginning stages of wealth creation. Most people say, "I don't have money to save," then they wake up twenty years later saying the same thing. Saving money is like working out—you have to force the habit. Once you force the habit, it will become a way of life. The way you save will evolve as you grow.

Avoid credit-card debt, student-loan debt, or any type of debt, unless what you are borrowing will help you make more money. Do not accumulate liabilities; build assets. A liability, to me, is any purchase that is worth less money than the purchase price one year later. Don't try to keep up with the Joneses because the Joneses are *broke*! (SMH). When you are saving money, you walk and talk differently, and people respond to you differently.

See and feel yourself building money. See and feel yourself creating wealth. Once you accumulate money, then you can start spending money on the things that create happiness for you and your family

Budgeting. Your budget should consist of the following categories:

1. Personal bills
2. Business bills
3. Personal expenses
4. Business expenses
5. Savings
6. Entertainment
7. Miscellaneous—miscellaneous can be charity, donations, clothing, etc.
    (see below budget worksheet)

Monthly Budget for the Month of

A budget can help you reduce your debt and save for goals.

Income	Budget Amount	Actual Amount	Difference	Notes
Income				
Income Total				
Other Income				

Expenses				
Mortgage/Rent				
Household Maintenance				
Taxes				
Insurance				
Electricity				
Water				
Sewage				

Gas				
Phone				
Trash				
Cable				
Cell Phone				
Groceries				
Entertainment				
Charity/ Donations				
Fuel				
Auto insurance				
Car Payment				
Child Care				
Credit Cards/ Debt				
Loans				
Life Insurance				
Health Insurance				
Clothing				
Child Support/ Alimony				
Other				

Savings				
Retirement				
College				
Basic/Other				

Savings. If you save your money, one day your money will save you. There are three categories of savings I always do my best to maintain:

1. *Emergency Fund.* One should always be put aside in case of unforeseen situations. One thing about life is that things will always occur were money is needed. If financial emergencies arise, and you do not have the money, it is a big challenge. If you have the money, it is only a resolvable situation. Emergency funds should be put in an instrument where you can access the money within twenty-four hours.

2. *Short-Term Goals.* Saving money for short-term goals can be identified as any item you want to purchase or achieve within a one to two-year period of time. Short-term goals could be:
   a)   purchasing a car
   b)   investing in a business
   c)   purchasing a home
   d)   taking a vacation

3. *Long-Term Goals.* Most of my long-term savings are focused on instruments that could help me build financial freedom by creating opportunities where I can have residual income. Some of the vehicles used to accomplish freedom are:
   a)   mutual funds
   b)   stocks—most of my portfolio are high-dividend-producing companies
   c)   variable annuities—tax deferred
   d)   investing in my businesses
   e)   owning real estate

Five Stages of Wealth Creation

1. I believe the first step is to identify a business you want to get involved with. You can start part-time or full-time. The business can be cutting hair, marketing a product, providing a solution to today's challenges, or cutting grass; something that can help you develop the habit and mindset of being independent. Most successful business owners may have started part-time then transitioned to full-time. Starting part-time allows you the opportunity to

earn while you learn without the initial pressure of being full-time. Once you go full-time, you would have gained the experience of running a business. Remember whatever you decide to do, give it everything you have. I started my first business adventure when I was eighteen years old. I started my financial service business at age twenty-two. I went full-time after two years. When I was part-time in business, while still serving in the US Navy, I treated my business like I was full-time. I acted like I did not have my Military pay coming in. I forced myself to substitute my income even though I was a single parent. I found a way to raise my sons and build a business. I took all my sons on appointments with me. They all watched me sacrifice to be successful. I had no doubt that I would make it! Beginning part-time first gave me the confidence that I could *win*!

2. Increase your cash flow. The reason I went into business for myself was to increase my earning potential in order to accomplish my goals. Some people say they have a business, but they do not generate revenue. This is very important if you are going to invest your valuable time into anything—you must make it worth it. Money is not the most important thing. However, it has to be one of the top priorities. No one will take you seriously if you are not making money. When I was broke, everyone knew it: the gas station attendant, the dry cleaners, and the restaurants where I ate. I never liked that feeling. I made up my mind that I had to get paid for my efforts. I figured out how much I needed to:

    a) pay my bills
    b) save to reach my goals
    c) have fun!

    I did this while part-time in business. By doing this, it gave me a since of urgency and provided a specific dollar amount to focus on.

3. Start investing in a diversified conservative portfolio, even if you have to start with $50 per month. Mutual funds

were my portfolio of choice. Once I invested for about one to two years, I began understanding how money worked. I later started an individual stock portfolio of high-dividend-paying stocks.

4. Real estate. Once you have started accumulating money and have about $150,000-plus saved, you should consider buying low-priced homes in an up-and-coming neighborhood. I recommend that you buy and hold instead of flip. Buy and hold gives you the ability to create residual income for a sustained period of time. I paid cash for some of my homes because I did not want to create additional debt. Buying homes was another means of asset accumulation without the high risk of investing in the stock market. You can start small and slowly accumulate a portfolio of homes. Never rush success. Walk it down with an intense focus.

5. Diversify your business. Start creating multiple sources of revenue. Once you have totally focused on building one business and you have saved money and created assets, continue building liquid assets. As your liquid assets grow, have your assets work for you. You don't have to know exactly what other business you want to build or invest in now. As you are in the middle of the wealth-building stages and you continue to work on your mind, the vision will come to you when you least expect it. *Build a business, save your money, then build your money.*

CHAPTER 5

What It Takes to Become an Entrepreneur

It's the thought of the thing, not the thing itself, that's the most difficult!
—TB

HOW TO GO into business for yourself/how to start:

- Make a decision.
- Seek mentors.
- Determine what it will cost to start.
- Create a marketing strategy.
- Understand your market.
- Build a team.
- Create capital.

Make a Decision: On what you would like to accomplish, trying to decide what you want to accomplish or what type of business you want to start is the key. Dig deep inside yourself and work on figuring out what type of goods or services that you feel can be beneficial to others, as well as something that's marketable. You can be innovative and create a new idea or use an existing system and buy into that. Don't get frustrated if you do not have a solid solution at this point. Having a desire will help you manifest your dream. Decide if you want to start your business *part-time* or *go full force*.

Seek Mentorship: Once you decide on what, it is critical to seek out individuals that have had success in your field. Don't be afraid to ask for advice. Be careful not to ask someone that has never been in business. Remember your drive and dreams are different from most (you are a ten percenter's). Mentorship can come in different forms. You can get mentorship by asking successful people in your field for advice. Study the history of successful people. Find out what helped them succeed. Study people that may have failed so you can learn what not to do.

Create a mastermind group—a group of individuals that are like-minded. Spend time with your mastermind group and meet with them or talk with them at least once a week. Take vision trips at least four to six times yearly. This will help you stay in tune with focused individuals that have the same desires to succeed. Avoid negative-thinking people at all costs. It's very difficult to overcome a negative environment. The internet is my savior; whatever I need to research I can find it on the World Wide Web. *Study*!

Determine your start-up cost. Do detailed research. Find out exactly how much up-front money you will need to start your business. Things you need to consider:

    a)   Materials or supplies needed
    b)   Licensing or patent if needed
    c)   Staff if needed
    d)   Overhead/office-space expense
    e)   Emergency reserve needed

Understanding your Market and Create a Marketing Strategy

Define in the beginning what your demographics is/ what your target market is.

When I started my first business, our market was clear—middle American families. We had a five-point approach. We focused on individuals that were:

a) married
b) homeowners
c) with kids
d) core ages 25–65
e) $25,000+ annual income

Those who stayed in that market were the most profitable and ultimately became the most successful.

My construction company philosophy was, we wanted to target homeowners but limit direct initial exposure, so we marketed to the main source that dealt with the most homeowners. We developed an intense market strategy. We felt if we could penetrate the source, we could get to the homeowner. Today 90 percent of our business is generated from a third-party referral.

Marketing. One of the most important aspects of starting a business is marketing. With a sound marketing plan, you can create a powerful opportunity for growth. Despite what people may think, marketing does not have to cost a lot of capital. There are several inexpensive ways to penetrate the marketplace. Below are some of the strategies I used to launch my business.

1) *Warm Market.* Call around to all of your family, friends, and associates. Ask them to give you the opportunity to meet for twenty minutes to explain your concept and to see if they feel it can be helpful to people they may know. If you have 150 referrals and 50 percent give you the opportunity to meet, that's seventy-five potentials; and if 50 percent of the seventy-five give you five referrals, that's another 187 people you have the opportunity to share your business with.

2) *Business to Business.* I went to businesses in my city and let them know what we were doing. I dropped off brochures,

introduced myself, and got their contact information. I compiled a database for future follow-up.

3) *Internet Research.* We researched all businesses that could use our services or businesses that had clients that could utilize our products. We compiled a database from there and did intense marketing.

4) *Email Marketing.* Once we developed our database, we created an attractive flyer with all our services, our contact information, and our mission. We sent out e-mails every day for ninety days. We developed a new list every day. Once we started making solid connections and started doing business with these prospects, our business grew expeditiously. It took us less than three years to start producing one million dollars in revenue.

5) *Social Media.* Social media is effective after you have established your brand. Social media, we feel, is used to keep the exposure going to keep the brand strong and relevant. We don't recommend startup companies spend a lot of resources and time on social media in the beginning stages.

6) *Word of Mouth.* Do your best to do your best, and people will start coming for your services. Although, you will never please everyone. However, if your intentions are right and you're providing a good-quality service to the public, it will not go unnoticed.

Building a Team. In order to have longevity and freedom, you must build a team. Building a team is challenging because you have to recruit people to your vision. You have to get them to believe that you have a service that can help the community and help them. When recruiting people to your organization, you must always present the concept as to how it can help others and how they can fit into the process. Never sell yourself.

All businesses that I started, once I had the concept and vision clarified, I scheduled a group meeting with individuals that I felt could benefit from coming into business with me. I needed the proper staff in place to support our mission.

In order to grow your business, you must grow people. You must always make others feel their value to the organization. I believe in the concept of giving everyone the feeling as if they have a sense of ownership. With my construction business, I always make the lead person on-site feel like they are in charge even when I come to inspect the sites. I would never communicate with the workers; I would deal directly with the leader, and if there were issues that needed to be addressed, I would not discuss them in front of their team. If a leader would start venting any frustration or rebuttal in front of their team, I would inform them not to do so. With my financial-service business, I had up-line leaders that were above me. I would be 100 percent coachable to those leaders. I never discussed my disapproval in any way to my subordinates. When building a team, you must always show unity. *(Growth cannot occur in the midst of conflict.)*

Creating Capital. This is a very important component of building a business. I did not have to apply for loans to start my business because I always started part-time. While I was part-time in business, I learned how to not only build a business effectively. I saved money to expand my business.

My journey to entrepreneurship started while in the military. When I was at sea for nine months at a time, I became creative. Because I didn't like the way the barbers cut my hair, I decided to start cutting my own. I was terrible at first but got better as time went on. One day I was cutting my hair, and one of my shipmates asked if I could cut theirs as well, and I said sure. I assumed I did a good job because more shipmates were asking if I could cut their hair as well. I was not charging at first, but as the demand increased, I started charging for my services. Within a short period of time I had people lined up outside of the bathroom for haircuts. All the money I made, I saved. When we docked in Naples, Italy, there was a location called Thieves Ally; it was full of designer suits, shoes, watches, and all. Once I witnessed this, I had a vision of loading up merchandise and selling to the sailors.

I also created a money-lending business. When we hit port, most sailors would spend all their money drinking or sending it home to their families; they never had extra funds. They would come to me and borrow money and pay it back with interest on payday. It was a revolving cycle. If I loaned $20, they would have to pay back $25. If it was a $30 loan, they would have to pay back $40. The higher the loan, the more they had to pay back. I had people on the ship that would come to my self-made barbershop on Sundays. I had another group that was interested in changing up their wardrobe that would purchase my merchandise and another group that would borrow money. So, with these entities, I created my own three-tier enterprise.

All debts had to be cleared before we hit our homeport in Norfolk, Virginia. One cruise I only cashed one of my military checks because I had so much revenue coming in I didn't need the funds. I would save most of the money I made with a plan to open a store one day. If you really think about it, it is simple to make money in America. Find a need and market the solution to that need.

Evolution of Capital Creation

- Cut hair on the ship while in the Navy
- Sold fashion merchandise while in the Navy
- Started my financial services business part-time while in the Navy
- Saved money while doing all the above businesses part-time
- Went full-time and built my financial-services business; total focus for seven years
- *Built capital*
- Used the capital I saved from my financial services business to start my construction company
- Saved more capital from the construction-company revenue
- Used the capital from my construction company to pay cash for my real estate investment properties

Start small, raise capital, and use your capital to expand

When we hear something, we may forget it!
When we see something, we may remember it!
But not until we do something is when we truly understand it!

CHAPTER 6

Leadership Principles of Million-Dollar Earners

*Don't judge your future success
on your struggles of today.*

BEING SUCCESSFUL AND building a business require leadership. Having the ability to affectively empower others, to buy into your vision, to buy into your management philosophy is a profound attribute.

This chapter, on leadership, is dedicated to some of the most successful people I personally know. We will provide principles from these powerful individuals. I strongly believe all the enclosed principles will give you the ammunition to build a strong operation.

1. Limit the need to show control. In order to empower others, you must make them feel as if they are an important part of the mission. (Tauheed S. Burke)
2. No man will be a great leader who wants to do it all himself or to get all the credit for doing it. (Andrew Carnegie)
3. There are risk and cost to action, but they're far less than the long-range risk of comfortable inaction. (John Kennedy)
4. It's fine to celebrate success, but it's more important to heed the lessons of failure. (Bill Gates)

5. Use your life to serve the world, and you will find that it will also serve you. (Oprah Winfrey)
6. All successful people I know, when not working, have something that stimulates their mind, something the soothes them. The act of the mind stimulation intensifies their desire to win. (Tauheed Burke)
7. *Joseph Ward* leadership principles:
   Leaders should:
   - have *consistent, clear communication* with their team at all times;
   - create a *positive structured environment* for growth; and
   - create high *expectations* linked to *personal development.*
8. *Sedrick Thomas* leadership principles:
   - What we think, we speak; what we speak, we believe; what we believe, we create.
   - Personal self-development is key to next-level achievement; we grow personally by reading books.
   - Listen to leaders that have an obtained success.
   - Attend seminars and lectures on topics of interest.
   - You must pay the price for success in your daily disciplines and give your efforts time enough to compound.

To achieve your goals, you will endure some challenges. Powerful individuals like Peggy Hightower, John Lennon, W. F. Chesley, Ivan Earle, and Andy Young impacted my life as I built my businesses. Each are successful. Each make at least one million dollars a year. They share *their early struggles in their business-development process and leadership principles that helped build success. Special bonus addition of one of the greatest leaders of our generation: Five leadership qualities of Kobe Bryant.*

Ivan Earle, National Sales Director

Ivan Earle, a prominent leader in American business, like so many, had to overcome many hurdles in order to achieve success. For him, his biggest struggle early on was making a conscious decision that in order to succeed, he had to roll up his sleeves and go to *work*.

So many times Ivan watched as his business colleagues worked diligently for six and sometimes seven days per week while he was putting in about three days a week. He watched as their income grew while his stayed the same or decreased. Over time he came to the understanding that he had to adopt the mentality that working harder delivers results. He found out that complacency was holding him back from growth. When he made up his mind to work longer, harder, and smarter, he saw his business grow and income increase. It takes discipline and a strong will to overcome the hurdles of being comfortable. Earle encourages people to take that first step: work hard and avoid complacency!

Ivan reflected on what factors helped propel him to success. For many years he would "do it all" himself. It did not take him long to discover that in order to "build sustainable and long-term financial independence, you cannot do it alone. You must train and develop others to do what you do. Build a strong leadership team and watch your cash flow grow. When you build a team and you do it well, you will become *successful*."

With over thirty years of success in business, Ivan Earle attaches himself to four principles of success, which has guided him along the way:

- Work eight hours a day to survive. Work over eight hours a day to succeed.
- What the mind can conceive, the body will achieve.
- Life is not about what happens to you but how you react to it; positive or negative—that's a choice that you have to make.

We all get knocked down in life. The key to success is how you get back up.

Peggy Hightower, National Sales Director

For Peggy Hightower, graduating from college was important to her parents. Growing up in the Maryland / Virginia / Washington, DC, area, she was the youngest of five children and the only one in her immediate family to go to college. Her parents were excited! This *determination* to *succeed, at college or anything in life,* was developed early on with the support of her family. Because of her passion to help others, she became a registered nurse. Being a single parent of two kids, she always had a desire for more. At her nursing job, she went to work early and stayed late and saw little in the way of financial growth. She became frustrated and began researching to find out how to achieve more for her family.

An opportunity presented itself by which she could make money part-time, working around her schedule with the opportunity to build a business. At first, she said "no" to the opportunity, but eventually, after pondering her desire to increase her income, she considered the transition. *What influenced her decision to accept the new journey?* She realized that she could still help heal others by healing their financial challenges and her desire to seek financial independence and build a legacy for her kids.

While in the middle of building her business, Peggy later married Eric Hightower, and together they worked hard and diligently. As a person of strong faith, she sought God for continued guidance as they were building. For her, it is important that people know their "why/reason" in order to stay focused. She stated, "You need to be asking and seeking what you believe in." Early on, like so many, there were challenges—the struggle of little to no income when starting a new business and making sure household bills were being paid. *The first six months were difficult, but the Hightowers realized that if they paid the price now, they would reap the benefits later!*

Peggy and Eric started building a team of like-minded individuals. Despite the setbacks, they continued to push forward. Within two years they opened their first office. Before achieving that level, the struggles of supporting a young family while building a business was challenging economically, but they endured. They wanted to be financially free and built from the concept of helping others become free financially. *What propelled them was a desire to build a legacy and help others build their own legacy.*

During the journey to financial independence, the Hightowers faced a devastating blow. Their home went into foreclosure. She fell on her knees and cried out to God for help. Instead of giving up, they decided to continue to focus on their goals. It took about two years to regroup. A few years later, she and her husband opened more offices and their income rose to $500,000. *She held on to her fundamental principle that "people need to become free!"* She wanted a team who shared that belief and was willing to work hard to achieve that same principle. Her goal was now to become the first African-American female in the financial service company to reach $100,000,000 a year in personal cash flow. The desire was there, and she was willing to pay the price to get there.

In 2015 the plans got sidetracked again. This time, Peggy's number-one teammate and life partner, Eric Hightower, died, and it took Peggy two more years to get her "sea legs" back, she stated. Her now-mature and determined leadership group vowed to lead the charge while Peggy was getting herself back together. The leaders continued to growth the business and develop new leaders. Peggy continued to speak at conferences and work toward her goal of becoming a million-dollar earner. For her, it's not easy; it's just worth it! *"Get strong in the dark hour.* You will take hits as you build. The objective is to keep winning while taking those hits."

With her growth in income, Ms. Hightower traveled to such places as Cairo, Egypt. She opened more offices in Texas, North Carolina, and Alabama, with strong teams in place to build their own legacies! *She paid the price of success by ending a stable career by most standards and stepped out in faith to pave a way for others to build financial freedom!*

With continued faith and a passion for helping people, Peggy Hightower is a trailblazer in her own right. Like so many, there were doubters of her vision. For her, her motivation was her *"why?"* She encourages people to be sold out to their *why* so they will fully commit to their end goal. Her love of God and strong commitment to family and community allowed her to recently achieve her goal of becoming the first African-American female in her financial-services firm to make over one million dollars in income! Her vision was met, and she paid the price through hard work, dedication, and family support. As she so wonderfully stated, "Fulfillment comes in building a business." Without a doubt, she has done just that and is an inspiration to millions! I am very proud of her and am happy for the positive impact she has made in my life.

John Lennon, National Sales Director

How many of us can look back at our life and pinpoint the people, or person, who greatly impacted our life? For John Lennon, a financial-services-industry leader, the answer comes easy—his father.

Lennon grew up on a small farm owned by his father in the eastern part of North Carolina. Unlike so many others who were sharecroppers, he owned his land. His mother was a teacher, and his father tended to the farm. The farm yielded such crops as cotton, tobacco, peanuts, and peaches. His father made a living selling the produce from the farm intown. As a boy, John watched his father work hard but did not equate what his father was doing with the concept of "building and running" a business. He only saw it as hard labor. In his later life, his reflection of that was pivotal on his path to success. *Watching his parents work hard helped him develop the determination to succeed!*

After high school, it was a given that John would go to college. He enrolled in North Carolina A&T State University in Greensboro, North Carolina. His initial plan was to major in Math because he excelled in that subject. Once he got into college and "understood what accounting was all about," he switched his major and received his BS in accounting.

While in college, he went into business for himself, "emulating" the work ethics he saw as he watched his father. Besides owning a farm, his father had a dry-cleaning business whereby he would take his clients clothes to the city. He had a contract with one of the local cleaners. Because most of them lived in rural farming communities and didn't have transportation, Mr. Lennon would handle all the deliveries and would charge a fee for service. If it cost a dollar to get a pair of pants cleaned, he would charge his client $1.25 or $1.50. "I saw how my dad made money managing a farm and a dry-cleaning company, and that left a lasting impression on me."

Taking after his father, while in college he started a cleaning business as well. During the early sixties, while in college, utilizing his truck, John would take students clothing to the cleaners for a small fee. It became "very profitable." In addition, he had a "landscaping business" He would go door to door and introduce himself: "Hello, my name is John Lennon. I am a student at A&T North Carolina working my way through college. My purpose here today is to see if you will allow me to cut your grass and trim your hedges." He employed others to do the labor, and he built up the clientele. He was able to build a profitable business using the lessons taught to him by his father. His father did not believe in debt, and he instilled that in his son. He would face a challenge that put his father's feelings about debt to the test.

While he was in college, John married Angela Lennon, the love of his life. They later had four children. To support his new family, John then decided to get into the real estate business. He heard he could make good money in real estate, and he figured it would be a great opportunity. He and some other men went into business together. Things were going well...until they weren't. His partners were more "astute" in business. Him being new to it, he didn't pay close attention to the details. The business was making money, and the partners paid themselves and him. However, they never paid taxes! Worst of all, his "friends" left him, alone, holding the empty bag, owing the IRS a total of $400,000!

Those were challenging times. With a wife and children, he needed to find a way to get out of debt and secure a future for his family. In 1979 he met someone who introduced him to the financial services industry. With his background in math and accounting, he felt this would be a way to build a business and overcome this huge debt. Another challenge for him was, although he understood numbers, he felt he had no experience in building people.

For the next ten years, while struggling to build a business and learning how to build people, he created a passion to build a legacy of generational wealth for his family and throughout the country. Using the concepts he was taught, he heeded his father's warning about debt. John set out to eliminate the $400,000 debt. *To set things in motion, he formulated an essential, fundamental principle for himself that continues to serve him well today: "Save 10 percent of your money off the top. Pay yourself first, and all others will fall into place."*

By continuing to build his business, mentor others, and build teams of people who wanted the same financial freedom, he was able to become debt free and financially independent. *He saved and accumulated money.*

John C. Lennon's leadership principles:

- Build people and understand how to leverage their efforts.
- Devise a plan not to sell but to engage others to do what you are doing and leverage that.
- A business is separate from its owner. Learn the difference.
- Discipline and focus are key to obtaining financial independence.
- Love the game and share that concept.
- If you want to change your life, build a constant and continuous stream of income.

John Lennon is a titan in the financial-services field. To get there, he paid the price to achieve success. He endured bankruptcy and times of having little money to support his family. He has been a million-dollar-plus earner for several years and is benefiting from the early lessons he learned from his father and building through his challenges. At times, when he wanted to give up, he kept on going, kept on fighting, kept on building. For him, a legacy is the end result "of having a game plan and process in place." He encourages us all to focus, build, and become financially independent!

Andy Young, National Sales Director

Born in Oxon Hill, Maryland, Andy Young gravitated toward football at a young age. Living fairly close to RFK Stadium, home field of the Washington Redskins football team, his love of the game and competitive nature played a major role in his path to success.

Andy came from a loving and supportive family. Many times they struggled to make ends meet, so he felt the need, at a young age, to pitch in. His mother being disabled, he felt even more compelled to find different ways to bring money into the home. He started cutting grass to chip in. Due to his mother's physical limitations, he learned how "to sew, cook, and maintain a household." *Those early skills helped him to understand that in order to succeed, "you have to figure a way to survive...find a way to* win!"

Andy's desire was to be the best in the game. To be the best, Young felt that "you have to *shadow* the best." *When asked where that determination came from, he said, "It just came from within. I can't really pinpoint where. It was just natural, I guess. I always wanted better than I had, and for me to do that, I had to go out and do it. I had to do what the best did and do it...sometimes better."* He was determined to succeed at whatever he did. That mantra still follows him today.

As a standout athlete, Andy's stature earned him a football scholarship to Wake Forest Univ. His dream was to play in the NFL. He asked himself, "How can I get better?" His answer: With grit and determination; with that mindset, he found a way to work out with one of the Redskins players. He studied his movements; he paid attention to the nuances easily overlooked by most. For him, this study was just another step on his journey to Greatness. However, adversity hit. He was playing in front of over fifty thousand people. NFL scouts all in the stands and just like that, his dreams of playing professional football ended on one play. He severally damaged his leg and never to play football again. He eventually, after five years, graduated from college.

Not knowing his next move, an opportunity presented itself; and true to form and his nature, Young jumped at the opportunity to immerse himself in Spanish. Most people study it in school and are comfortable with that. Others travel abroad and return, shortly thereafter, proud of what they have learned; not Andy Young. He went to Columbia and lived among the people so that he could be *successful* at understanding and communicating at a proficient level. Again, Andy's motto is "learn from the best to become the best. To become big, you have to get into the environment where you shadow the person you want to be."

When he returned to the United States, opportunities presented themselves, especially with his bilingual ability. He worked at different jobs but was not making the kind of money he felt he needed to reach his goal of financial independence. One day the right opportunity presented itself, and the journey into entrepreneurship begun.

As he embarked on building his business, he read, he attended meetings, he planned, planned and planned. In order for his business to grow, he had to find like-minded people who wanted to succeed at any cost. He had little to no money. His struggles were real. Sometimes he slept on floors; sometimes he slept in his car. *The leaders in his industry who had succeeded encouraged him throughout his journey. He felt that if others could succeed, he could as well.*

Andy became a regional vice president and moved back to Maryland. One of the first things he did with his team was map out the Washington, DC, Maryland, Virginia area. He pointed out all the location where he wanted to set up offices. His goal was to help others build a business open office and help individuals become financially. He painted a picture of future success for not only himself but for all that would be involved in his business.

Day in and day out, struggling and putting in the work, he slowly began to see growth. He and some of his team members would pile into a car and travel to Atlanta to attend meetings and conferences. As his business grew and his income increased, he was able to send a couple of vanloads to Atlanta. He was determined to make sure his team found ways to be in an environment of success. Before he knew it, busloads were going to the conferences.

That principle, to become better and to get the best out of people, continued to pave his way to success. There were doubters, but that inner drive to do something special for his family kept him going. As Andy's business grew, his income grew. He was, and still is, a firm believer "in building people" and "keeping them in a winning environment where they can emulate successful people."

Because of his willingness to "pay the price" and sacrificing, his income is among the highest in the financial-services industry. He has produced over one hundred people making over 100,000 per year. He has five people making one million or more per year. When he started making a six-figure income, he flew his parents to Hawaii. His mother wanted to go to Hawaii because it was the last place her brother was before he died in war. It was a trip she never has forgotten. Because he paid the price of success, he was *easily* able to afford that trip…and countless others.

Andy Youngs leadership principles:

- Winners win and losers lose.
- Nothing is ever sold out, and all restaurants are all you can eat.
- Recruiting is the key to growth in any business.
- You must expand your teammates/leaders' vision.
- Keep your teammates/leaders in a competitive environment if you want growth.
- Of all the things I've ever said, the things I'm most proud of are the things I never said.
- Always get a good night's sleep before making impulsive and emotional decisions.
- If you need gratitude from anyone, get a dog; they'll always be happy to see you. If you're really needy, get two.

There are so many Andy Youngs in the making. He had nothing special other than a determination to achieve a better life for his family. Sleeping on floors and his car were struggles he went through to achieve financial freedom and to help others become financially free. Andy Young from Oxon Hill, Maryland, is now a tycoon in American business.

W. F. Chesley Sr. Owner of Chesley Realty

Mr. W. F. Chesley, known as Bill Chesley, grew up in Chillum, Maryland. Getting married as a teenager in order to support his family, he was forced to get a job instead of going to college. He started his real estate business part-time as an agent in 1970. He didn't sell his first home until after three months of struggling to understand sales. He stated, "I worked hard enough until I got good enough." As he and his business grew, he bought lots, he started building homes, and later became a developer. Forty-nine years later his company is still one of the top firms in the DC metropolitan area. Mr. Chesley is known for developing the well-known community in Prince George's County, *The Perry Wood Estates,* a 1400 hundred home community. He bought the land in 1980, and it took ten years to start building. In 1993 the community started being develop.

Mr. Chesley watched his parents work extremely hard. He admired their discipline. He eventually moved with his grandparents in St. Mary's County, Maryland. His grandparents owned a farm. He watched them get up early and work late every day. As a child, he witnessed that working hard was a way of life in his family and throughout the community he was raised. While growing up on a farm, Bill stated although they had no electricity or heat; they heated their home with a woodburning fireplace. His grandparents always had a good meal prepared. As he got older, he realized that his grandparents had very little. However, he said to himself, "We were never poor as long as we had three meals a day." Chesley was a below-average student; however, playing sports was a contributing factor to his development. He said they got rewarded for winning. His coach created a winning habit within him. During the time Bill played sports, they were able to practice all year; and when they were not practicing, he stated he would be at the gym working out. His coach told him winners should feel bad about losing. The discipline of sports is what you will need to Win (W. F. Chesley).

In his early days of trying to build his business, a successful sales person came to his office.

Mr. Chesley asked, "What is the key to your success?"

The salesman leaned back and said, "I am lucky."

Mr. Chesley again asked, "Why are you so lucky?"

The salesman said, "It's funny. The harder I work, the luckier I get." He stated, "Most unlucky people are not willing to work."

Mr. Chesley then told me, "People are dying all over the world to be free. We are living her in America, in the nation's capital. That's lucky enough. But yet most people refuse to work hard on their goals and dreams."

Below are some of Mr. Chesley's leadership principles:

- Earn while you learn.
- Listen to what others are saying; pay attention.
- Do what you say you are going to do.
- Work every day until 9 PM to succeed.
- You can do anything you want to do if you're willing to work hard enough.
- Always be, friendly, courteous, and respectful.
- It's not hard to be successful; it's hard to deal with failure. During your journey, you will fail.
- To survive the tough times, you must be conservative.
- Don't build debt.
- You don't have to be special to succeed
- Be honest, and your business will grow.

At age seventy-six W. F. Chesley is still actively getting dressed up with a suit and tie and going to his office every day, working out, and playing soccer. His final statements were: It's not money that drives me. It's being able to help others in need; you can make others happy. The habit of winning and sacrificing. It's a feeling of self-worth. Because money goes away at the end for all of us.

Leadership Qualities of the Great: Kobe Bryant

1. *Meticulous Preparation*

No one in the NBA prepares for a game like Kobe Bryant. He spends endless hours studying game tape of the opposing team, his direct match-ups(s), team match-ups, and everything else in a bid to understand and counter what the opposition has to offer. Kobe understood from an early age, the importance that preparation had on how he performed on the court. This was in part due to his self-awareness that he could not initially simply overpower anyone due to his then-slender frame. "I was a scrawny kid", he said. "I knew for me to get any type of edge whatsoever I had to be more prepared than the person I was matching up against." Not that being scrawny has been much of an issue for Kobe in the NBA—he has listed at 6'6'' (198cm) and around 215 pounds (97.5 kg) for most of his career and is one of the most physically gifted players of his generation. And yet his preparation for games has only gone up several notches since his rookie season, not only preparing pregame but during games as well. At half-time of games, Kobe would go back to the locker room to study game tape of the 1st half and would often get his teammates to watch examples of plays in preparation for the 2nd half.

Kobe's preparation is something that would make every professional better. No matter how talented or gifted you are, nothing beats preparation in obtaining excellent results—whatever it may be. If you want to smash that sales pitch, presentation, or client meeting—preparation is the key to success. Much like Kobe learns his opponent's game, preparation will allow you to learn who your audience is, understand your deliverable inside-out, and plan for any unexpected events that may be thrown at you. What I draw from Kobe is that preparation is how you will get the results, and those results aren't simply down to talent or luck, but hard work.

2.   *Strive for improvement*

Kobe Bryant was not a superstar overnight. He entered the NBA as an 18-year-old straight out of high school and experienced quite a few setbacks his first and second year of professional basketball. His four-straight air-balls against the Jazz in the 96-97 playoffs come to mind. However, Kobe also improved dramatically in those first couple of years, becoming arguably the best in his position and an NBA champion by his 4th year. His insatiable work ethic, ferocious competitive nature, and dedication as a student of the game made sure of that. Despite reaching the summit, Kobe continued to hone his game, spending endless summers watching and mimicking moves from NBA legends such as Michael Jordan, or improving his footwork with Hakeem Olajuwon to rely less on his diminishing athleticism to keep ahead of his competition.

Kobe's constant strive for improvement reminds me of the philosophy of 'Kaizen'; to continuously improve business processes, traditionally in manufacturing. Kobe's dedication to improvement is meticulous, and machine-like. This mentality is something that any professional can apply—to aim to continuously improve their craft; their clients, industries and markets, and to identify and illuminate waste in the way you do things (stop you tubing 2 hours a day!). To not be content (for too long) with the current skill set and knowledge that you possess because there is always something new to learn. To have the passion and curiosity to continuously learn and master is another. Look up the values and behaviors that are requisite to the large professional services firms and 'hunger to improve or grow' are commonplace.

Here's a quote on how Bryant wants to be remembered, which provides a great insight into his focus on getting the most out of himself: "To think of me as a person that's overachieved, that would mean a lot to me. That means I put a lot of work in and squeezed every ounce of juice out of this orange that I could."

3. *Resilience*

Throughout the years, Kobe Bryant has had his fair share of critics. The critics come far and wide, critiquing his performance from on the court and off it too. This has to be very exhausting and distracting for Kobe Bryant, especially when the criticism is warranted. But you really couldn't tell, given the magnificent seasons Kobe has provided and the championships he has delivered. Kobe Bryant, had a possible career ending Achilles injury. There have been few players who have been able to return to the court successfully after a torn Achilles tendon, especially a player of Kobe's age. This may have been Kobe's darkest hour as a player, and despite some initial disappointment, Kobe responded by vowing to study the recoveries of others who have suffered the injury to make the fastest and best recovery from an Achilles injury possible. Four months into his recovery, Bryant said that he has "shattered" the average recovery time from surgery. Bryant's resilience to the extreme challenges that he faced was his was amazing competitive advantage, where others would have buckled; he seemed to relish the challenge.

In an ever-changing world, every professional will go through a period of heightened stress where negative thoughts dominate and cloud the mind, severely handicapping performance. Your ability to quickly bounce back up and develop contingencies is one way of overcoming this, enabling you to keep performing at a high level regardless of the pressures and responsibilities encountered. Important in a time where presenteeism has cost Australian employers $34.1 billion in 2011. Another great benefit of building resilience is that your tolerance to stress can strengthen as the pressure grows— crucial as you climb the ladder, as you invariably take up larger roles, or sit in higher pressure environments. This is akin to seeing Bryant perform and excel in incrementally tougher stages—from the regular season, to the playoffs, and finally the finals, where championships are won and lost.

4.   *Leads by Example*

When you play for a team with Bryant beside you, you know you have someone that will stand up for the team when the going gets tough. Kobe will also strive to get the most out of you and each teammate, be it on the practice court, out of every timeout, and of course, during a game. Bryant will demand that you compete and give 110%,—anything less is unacceptable. He does this best by leading by example; he will only demand that you give as much as he gives. A rookie would learn much from training and playing with Kobe Bryant, as he is the king of the walk, and even if he blows his Achilles and can no longer walk, he still leads by example There is nothing more impressive to me than to see a leader practicing what he/she preaches, seeing your leader get down and do the hard yards to set the bar at where everyone else needs to be. Great leadership calls for a strong sense of accountability for not only getting the job done but also ensuring that those under your wing are given every chance to develop and shine. For someone at the early stages of his career, leaders that have this trait can really instill a lasting impression, and can really quickly change the working culture through their actions. This can quickly inspire a small project team or an entire workforce to strive to emulate at a minimum what they have seen as an example from their leader. Very, very few NBA champions or booming organizations have had poor leadership.

5.   *Self-belief*

All those qualities described above are relative without this one: self-belief. And Bryant h*ad* a truck-load of this. Bryant's belief in his own ability to push through and win games no matter the situation is legendary. You'd need a bit of self-belief to decide to bypass college for the NBA, challenge Shaq as the man on the Lakers, and ultimately lead your team to the championship five times. Witness his infinite belief in his ability and to his craft, through his incredible recovery from a torn Achilles at the moment— he was already running on a treadmill 4 months when the typical length of time is 6-9 months after a torn Achilles.

You can't do anything worthwhile without a little self-belief; it is the ultimate enabler to achieving great results. There have been numerous times where I rued that lost opportunity or failed to act in that moment because I didn't have the confidence to *just do it*. Self-belief allows you to take risks, and importantly buffer you from the setbacks that may come your way. It helps you to keep pushing, even if you have failed along the way. It is also important to distinguish self-belief from arrogance, as arrogance is characterized by a lack of self-awareness whereas self-belief requires self-awareness for it to be effective, and helps keep things in perspective, especially when you are not experiencing a linear journey towards your goals. This perspective is incredibly important to your ability to prepare, improve, lead, and block out the noise that distracts you from your objectives.

I have nothing in common with lazy people who blame others for their lack of success, Great things come from hard work and perseverance. *(Kobe Byrant)*

Succeed Anyway
People are illogical, unreasonable, and self-centered;
Love them anyway.
If you are kind, people may accuse you of selfish, ulterior motives;
Be kind anyway.
If you are successful, you will win false friends and true enemies;
Succeed anyway.
The good you do today will be forgotten tomorrow;
Do good anyway.
If you are honest and frank, people may cheat you;
Be honest and frank anyway.
The biggest men and women with the biggest ideas can be shot
down by the smallest men and women with the smallest minds;
Think big anyway.
What you spend years building may be destroyed overnight;
Build anyway.
If you find serenity and happiness, they may be jealous;
Be happy anyway.
People really need help but may attack you when you help them;
Help people anyway.
Give the world the best you have, and it may never be enough;
Give the world the best you've got anyway.
You see, in the final analysis, it is between you and your God;
It was never between you and them anyway. [*]

---

[*] Reportedly inscribed on the wall of Mother Teresa's children's home in Calcutta, and attributed to her. However, an article in the New York Times has since reported (March 8, 2002) that the original version of this poem was written by Kent M. Keith.

CHAPTER 7

Time goes by too fast to deny yourself a good quality of life.

AT THE END of every year, I take time to get away for fun, relaxation, and preparation. I usually go to a location that has an outstanding spa; somewhere peaceful and clam. At least one of the days on my yearly trip, I sit by myself and recap on my year. I then begin assessing what was accomplished for that year. I start creating a new theme and creating a new vision for the upcoming year. All that want to achieve success and happiness, write down your goals. Set goals in each of the below categories:

1. Spiritual
2. Physical
3. Family
4. Personal
5. Financial

I believe setting goals in these five areas of our lives will help create and maintain *happiness* and *purpose.*

When you encounter setbacks and disappointments, the one thing that will give you *hope* and *inspiration* will be your goals. Goals give you a reason to wake up and feel good about your life. Goals give you a reason to have a fresh start. Goals give you a reason to keep going when it seems impossible. Internalizing your goals will drive you to greater heights. You will be amazed at how far they will take you.

Decide What You Want in Life

A. Decide what you would like to accomplish short and long-term.
B. Decide what it will take to accomplish your goals.
C. What changes will you have to make to reach your goals?
D. What date would you like to accomplish each goal? (Decide on an exact date.)
E. How will you reward yourself or others for each accomplishment?

No one should want more for you then you want for yourself. Your one coach, cheerleader, and motivation should be you. Create a goal accountability worksheet. Print it, put it in a binder, and a copy should be by your bedside, your bathroom, and car. You should review your goal sheet every morning. All day and every night. If you do this the first thirty days in the beginning of the year, or whenever you start the process, you will store your goals in your subconscious mind, and your faculties will drive you toward what you desire. Yes, despite where you are physically, mentally, or financially, you can change your circumstances once you believe you can.

The following is my "Goal Accountability Worksheet" with explanations of each category:

Goal Accountability Worksheet			
Adjust your goals annually. As we grow mentally, our goals will evolve.			
Items to Obtain	*Price of Obtainment*	*Plan*	*Date of Accomplishment*
Notes:			

Goal Accountability Sheet Explanation

1. *Items to Obtain:*

   The column is used to write down all your goals you want to accomplish in the next twelve months from spiritual to financial.

2. *Price:*

   What is the cost to accomplish each goal written? (Example: If you need to pay off debt, you would write down the amount of the debt. If you want to save $5,000 in one year, you would list that amount. If you want to lose weight, write down the number of pounds you want to lose in three, six, and twelve months.)

3. *Plan:*

   What is the specific plan you will take to reach each goal? (Example: If your debt amount is $3,000 and you want to pay it off in twelve months, your plan would be to put $250 per month toward that goal. If you want to save $5,000 in twelve months, your plan would be to save $416.67 every month. If your goal were to lose seventy-eight pounds in three months, your plan would be to work out three times a week, stop eating beef and pork, and lose twenty-six pounds a month. Be very specific with your plan.)

4. *Date of Accomplishment*

   You must put specific dates you will accomplish your goals. (Example: If you want to pay off your debt, put the exact day it will happen. If you want to save $5,000, put the exact date it will happen. If you want to lose seventy-eight pounds in three months, indicate the exact date this will happen.)

   Fixating on specific goals followed by a specific plan and an exact date will help create the strategy and sense of urgency to make it happen.

5. *Notes*

Notes are used to write down the exact date you accomplished your goals. Notes are also used to jot down periodic activity, ideas, etc.

Things-to-Do Binder

One of the challenges that I find most people are having issues with is managing their daily schedule. We feel there is so much to do and very little time to accomplish. We get overwhelmed. Once a person gets overwhelmed, it cripples. To be a leader and become successful, you must be able to effectively manage your time and tasks.

I recommend buying a small five-by-eight notebook, keep it by your bedside at night, and carry it with you throughout the day. Write down your thoughts. Every night when you are home relaxing, assess your day and plan your attack for the next day. Write down all the important tasks that must be accomplished within the next twenty-four hours. Try not to focus on what's important next week. The most important day you have is now. Plan for the future and focus on the now. Once you jot down things to do for the upcoming twenty-four hours, e-mail it to your team/staff. Assign tasks to each staff member. Your personal task is to make sure you are on track. As we tackle the tasks, we draw a line through the completed items. Things to do lists help you have an organized approach to life.

~ The Beginning~

Acknowledgments

THANKS TO THE individuals who have been instrumental in my life...

- Darel "Man" Henson
- Buzzy Hicks
- Joseph Gray
- Theodus Dorsey
- Ivan Earle
- John Lennon
- Andy Young
- W. F. Chesley
- "Bullet" Bob Turley
- Last but not least, my mother, Estella Ewell

Special thanks to individuals who assisted in transmitting my vision...

- Maria Burke
- Catherine Peay
- April Miller

Bibliography

Andrew Carnegie—Edited 7 March 2020 at 3:58 (UTC) creative commons—Creative Commons Attribution-ShareAlike License wikimedia foundation inc

John f. Kennedy—Edited 17 March 2020 at 15:15 (UTC) creative commons—Creative Commons Attribution-ShareAlike License wikimedia foundation inc

Cesar Chavez—Edited 11 March 2020 at 3:29 (UTC) creative commons—Creative Commons Attribution-ShareAlike License wikimedia foundation inc

Base Reaves—Edited 12 March 2020 at 15:56 (UTC) creative commons—Creative Commons Attribution-ShareAlike License wikimedia foundation inc

"Kobe Bryant." SuitandJersy.wordpress.com/2015/11/26/5-qualities-Kobe_Bryant-possesses-that-will-make-you-better-professional/.

Madame CJ Walker—last edited on 24 March 2020, at 23:13 (UTC). Text is available under the Creative Commons Attribution-ShareAlike License wikimedia foundation inc

Black wall street—last edited on 20 July 2019, at 23:13 (UTC).Text is available under the creative commons—Creative Commons Attribution-ShareAlike License wikimedia foundation inc

About the Author

TAUHEED BURKE WAS raised in the inner city of Baltimore. Deep down he knew there was more to life. Throughout his struggles, he was determined not to end up like most. He fought his way out of the inner city, joined the United States Navy, and he began his journey to business ownership. He traveled the world and saw how great life could be if he paid the price to win. While in the Navy he started his first business. When leaving the military, he went full-time in business. The thought of working a job for someone else was not on his agenda. He had early success and then ran into major adversity. Through his adversity he got stronger. He built his financial-service business then used the capital to build his construction company and used the capital from his construction business and started buying properties to create more residual income. Tauheed now is a prominent figure in his community that raised him. He gives back to the inner city. He is a mentor and inspiration to many. He goes out his way to help teach others the principles that help him succeed. He has three awesome sons, Torrey, Tauheed, and Tahj; and two grandkids, Ms. Torri and Torran. He believes this book will change the way kids and young adults think about business ownership and money for generations to come.

www.ingramcontent.com/pod-product-compliance
Lightning Source LLC
Chambersburg PA
CBHW021504210526
45463CB00002B/880